MILITARY
ROBOTS

BY **BRETT S. MARTIN**

CONTENT CONSULTANT
Steven Shooter
Professor of Mechanical Engineering
Bucknell University

Core Library

An Imprint of Abdo Publishing
abdopublishing.com

Cover image: A member of the US Navy operates a
robot designed to disarm and destroy bombs.

abdopublishing.com

Published by Abdo Publishing, a division of ABDO, PO Box 398166, Minneapolis, Minnesota 55439. Copyright © 2019 by Abdo Consulting Group, Inc. International copyrights reserved in all countries. No part of this book may be reproduced in any form without written permission from the publisher. Core Library™ is a trademark and logo of Abdo Publishing.

Printed in the United States of America, North Mankato, Minnesota
022018
092018

Cover Photo: Gary Granger Jr./US Navy
Interior Photo: Gary Granger Jr./US Navy, 1; Ross Taylor/The Virginian-Pilot/AP Images, 4–5; Armando Babani/AP Images, 7; Iliya Pitalev/Sputnik/AP Images, 9, 45; William West/AFP/Getty Images, 12–13; US Navy/Interim Archives/ Archive Photos/Getty Images, 16, 43; Staff Sgt. J. R. Ruark/Department of Defense, 18; Rui Vieira/PA Wire URN:24024327/AP Images, 20–21; Army Alaska/US Army, 23; US Air Force/AP Images, 24 (top left); Erik Hildebrandt/Northrop Grumman/US Navy, 24 (top right); SPC. Michael J. MacLeod/Department of Defense, 24 (bottom left); PH2 (AW) Daniel J. McLain/DoD/Newscom, 24 (bottom right); Paul J. Richards/AFP/Getty Images, 27; Sergey Kohl/Shutterstock Images, 28–29; Vitaliy Belousov/Sputnik/AP Images, 31; Visual China Group/Getty Images, 33; Erik Hildebrandt/US Navy, 37

Editor: Bradley Cole
Imprint Designer: Maggie Villaume
Series Design Direction: Ryan Gale

Library of Congress Control Number: 2017962811

Publisher's Cataloging-in-Publication Data

Names: Martin, Brett S., author.
Title: Military robots / by Brett S. Martin.
Description: Minneapolis, Minnesota : Abdo Publishing, 2019. | Series: Robot innovations | Includes online resources and index.
Identifiers: ISBN 9781532114694 (lib.bdg.) | ISBN 9781532154522 (ebook)
Subjects: LCSH: Military robots--Juvenile literature. | Robotic soldiers--Juvenile literature. | Drone aircraft--Juvenile literature. | Military exoskeletons--Juvenile literature.
Classification: DDC 623--dc23

CONTENTS

CHANGING THE FACE OF WARFARE

The desert sun is scorching hot. Beads of sweat run down the soldiers' necks. The soldiers stop along a road outside of the city. They are part of a US Army Explosive Ordnance Disposal (EOD) unit. They are here to dispose of a roadside bomb planted in the ground. If someone were to drive by it, they could be killed.

Disarming bombs is a very dangerous job. The soldiers stay back a safe distance. They send the Talon. The Talon is a robot. It has

A member of an EOD unit observes a Talon IV robot in Iraq in 2010.

DESIGNING ROBOTS

BOMB DESTRUCTION SPECIALIST

In the 1990s, the US Army began using robots to get rid of bombs. The Talon is one of these robots. The Talon IV is the latest model. It weighs 168 pounds (76 kg). The Talon has brought a new way of thinking about military uses for robots. It's small, agile, and controlled with a remote. The Talon is also very durable. One was blown into a river by an explosion. It was driven out of the water and reused. Another one was damaged and then repaired 13 times.

cameras, sensors, and an arm that looks like a claw.

A soldier picks up a controller that looks like those used for video games. He steers the Talon toward the bomb. The Talon moves on tracks like a tank. Cameras let the operator see the explosive device.

High overhead, a Predator drone is circling. Like the Talon, this airborne robot is controlled remotely. Its cameras watch over the scene. At a distant air force base, a pilot is steering the

A US Predator drone can fly 135 miles per hour (217 km/h).

Predator remotely. He can warn the EOD unit if danger is nearby. Military drones can also take photos.

Back on the ground, the Talon operator nudges the remote control. In response, the Talon carefully places a small plastic explosive on top of the bomb. The Talon backs away. With everyone at a safe distance, a soldier presses a button. A loud explosion rips through the air. Dirt shoots skyward. The mission is a success. The plastic explosive blew up the bomb, making it harmless.

Whether in the sky or on the ground, robots are important military equipment. Advanced sensors help them navigate. Rugged designs keep them running in rough conditions. Highly skilled operators control them remotely. In today's military, robots help win battles and save lives.

ALL SHAPES, SIZES, AND ABILITIES

A robot is a machine programmed to perform certain tasks. Military robots are designed to assist and protect soldiers. They do jobs that would put soldiers' lives at risk. The Talon's ability to remotely destroy bombs is one example of this.

Each military robot is different. Robots can take pictures, launch weapons, walk like dogs, fly, or even swim. They can be small enough to fit in a soldier's hand or bigger than a car. Some even look like they belong in a science-fiction movie. One of the tiniest military robots is the Throwbot XT. Soldiers can toss it

Russia demonstrated the Uran-9 at a military show in 2017.

into hard-to-reach areas. Then they can drive it around remotely. One of the largest is Russia's Uran-9. It weighs more than 11 tons (10 metric tons). The Uran-9 has antitank missile launchers.

Robots come in many shapes and sizes. Still, they have some things in common. They can sense

THROWABLE ROBOTS

One of the smallest robots in the US Army is the Throwbot XT. It weighs just 1.2 pounds (540 g) and can be thrown up to 120 feet (35.5 m). Once it is tossed into a location, the soldiers can quietly scout the area. The robot sends video and audio to its operator. This lets the operator see inside rooms, behind walls, or into other dangerous areas.

their surroundings. They can move. And computer processors let them carry out a set of instructions. Many of today's robots are controlled by people. Some are able to make decisions on their own.

Military robots are unique among robots. They sometimes carry weapons. They can kill people. However, no country allows robots to make life-or-death decisions. A human must order a robot to fire its weapon. Someday, this might change. It is one of the biggest debates about military robots.

STRAIGHT TO THE
SOURCE

Christof Heyns gave a report to the United Nations Human Rights Council on robots that can kill people:

Lethal autonomous robotics (LARs) are weapon systems that, once activated, can select and engage targets without further human intervention. They raise far-reaching concerns about the protection of life during war and peace. This includes the question of the extent to which they can be programmed to comply with the requirements of international humanitarian law and the standards protecting life under international human rights law. . . . The [office] recommends that States establish national [bans] on aspects of LARs, and calls for the establishment of a high level panel on LARs to articulate a policy for the international community on the issue.

Source: Christof Heyns. "Report of the Special Rapporteur." *OHCR*. OHCHR, April 9, 2013. Web. Accessed October 17, 2017.

Consider Your Audience

Consider how you would adapt the passage for younger friends. Write a blog post conveying this same information for the new audience. How does your new approach differ from the original text, and why?

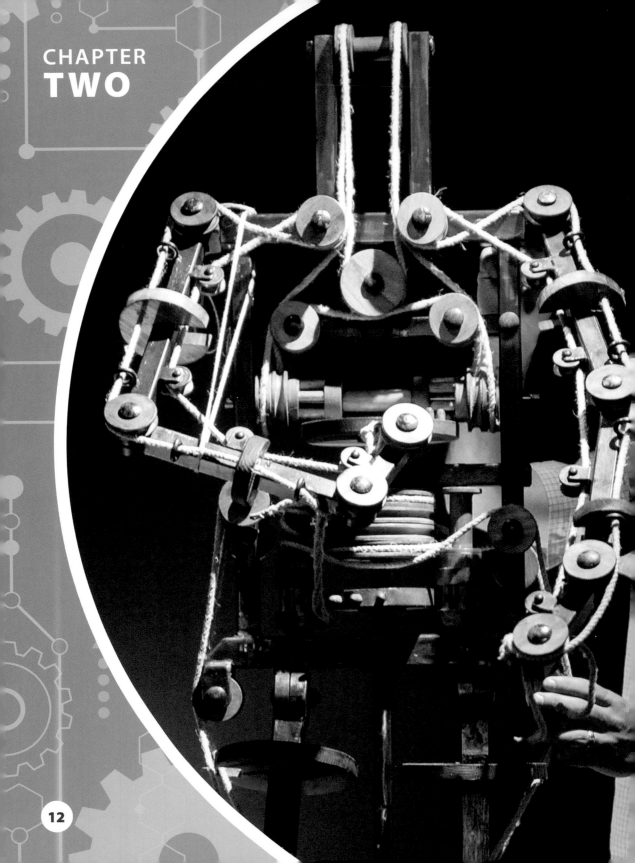

FROM DA VINCI TO MILITARY CONTRACTORS

The idea of using machines in the military is not new. The famous artist and inventor Leonardo da Vinci designed a mechanical knight in the mid-1490s. Cranks, cables, and pulleys would help the knight sit, stand, and turn its head. However, Leonardo's invention was intended for entertainment. It is unclear whether it was ever actually built.

A modern recreation of Leonardo's mechanical knight was on display in Melbourne, Australia, in 2009.

THE FIRST ROBOTIC BOAT

Remote-control technology has made new devices possible. Many of today's robots rely on it. Famed inventor Nikola Tesla created the first radio-controlled device in 1898.

He called his technology "teleautomaton." Tesla wanted to sell his idea to the US Navy. The navy didn't see the value and didn't buy it. However, remote-controlled devices were soon introduced to warfare. In World War I (1914–1918), the

German navy used remote-controlled boats with bombs to attack ships.

DESTRUCTIVE ROBOTS BECOME POPULAR

Robotics technology advanced by World War II (1939–1945). The Soviet Union developed the Teletank. It could be controlled from more than 0.6 miles (1 km) away. Operators pressed buttons on remote controls to steer it. The tank could also fire machine guns and use flamethrowers. If the tank drove out of range, it simply stopped. The operator would then get closer and it would start rolling again.

Germany also used robots during World War II. The Germans designed a remote-controlled vehicle called the Goliath. The tracked vehicle was knee-height. It could be loaded with 220 pounds (100 kg) of explosives. Then operators could steer it into tanks, buildings, and bridges. It was guided by a joystick control box.

The box was connected to the Goliath by long cables. Allied troops could stop the robot by cutting the cable.

ROBOTS TAKE TO THE SKY

Robots advanced after World War II. One major postwar development was the unmanned aerial vehicle (UAV). UAVs are now commonly called drones. In 1984, the US government gave $40 million to Leading Systems Inc., an aircraft company, to build a UAV.

Leading Systems named its first drone Amber. It was tested in 1986. Funding cuts spelled the end for the Amber. However, the technology and design

DRONES IN THE VIETNAM WAR

Military drones have received a lot of press coverage in recent years. That's because of their service in the Iraq War and the War in Afghanistan. However, they have been flying through the skies for more than half a century. In 1951, the Ryan Firebee could act like an airplane or missile. Fighter pilots used it to practice shooting down enemy planes and missiles.

US Navy troops examine a German Goliath in 1944.

The RQ-2 Pioneer drone saw use by the US military in the 1990s.

led to new drones. The RQ-2 Pioneer and RQ-5 Hunter were important steps in lightweight UAV design. The RQ-2 scouted for the US military in Bosnia in the 1990s.

Early drones were mostly used for scouting. Later they took on more roles. Fitting early drones with missiles required a lot of work. The missiles and launchers made the drones heavier. The force of the missile launching could also destroy the drone. To make this work required engineering and upgrades. Now they can even engage enemies. These improvements helped make robots more common in the Iraq War (2003–2011).

FURTHER EVIDENCE

Chapter Two discusses how military robots have changed through the years. What are some of the major advances in drone technology? Read the article at the website below. Does the information on the website support the main points of the chapter? What new information about drones does it cover?

ROBOT HISTORY: THE RISE OF THE DRONE
abdocorelibrary.com/military-robots

DESIGN IS A CONSTANT BATTLE

Building military robots requires advanced technologies. Drones must spend long hours in the air. They also must take high-quality pictures. Land robots must work in tough conditions. If robots break down, they can put soldiers' lives in danger. Developing robots can be expensive and slow. But the US military has heavily invested in this work. Engineers across the country are working to develop rugged and effective military robots.

Military robots, including drones, can be operated remotely. Some drones can be piloted from thousands of miles away.

KEEPING CONTROL

Robots face special challenges. If they stop working, they can be stuck until an operator can reach them. There is a solution. Some robots are designed to fix themselves. Other robots can adapt to keep working. In experiments, six-legged robots with two damaged legs could use their other legs to keep going.

Sometimes, drones are controlled from a base far away. The pilots sit in front of screens. They fly the drones from as far away as 7,000 miles (11,300 km). The US

AN ETHICAL DILEMMA

The use of robots on the battlefield raises ethical questions. Robots cannot reason the same way as humans. They could shoot missiles without thinking of the consequences. This is why humans control all military robots. The US government is spending millions of dollars to make human direction unnecessary. They want to create robots that understand moral choices. Robots would decide based on ethical reasoning, similar to humans.

Soldiers set up a robot control station in 2008 for a training mission in Valdez, Alaska.

military now has about 7,500 drones. They make up more than 40 percent of the military's aircraft.

Losing contact with a distant drone can be a serious problem. A drone could go out of control and crash. To prevent this, drones are told what to do if contact is lost. They may fly in circles or return to base.

US MILITARY
DRONES

These are four military UAVs. Drones can be small or very large, but they all cost a lot of money. How do you think having different sized UAVs with different capabilities can help the military in different ways?

Reaper MQ-9
Wingspan: 66 feet (20 m)
Flight time: 14 hours
Cost: $16.9 million
Use: Launches missiles; surveillance

Global Hawk RQ-4
Wingspan: 130.9 feet (39.8 m)
Flight time: 32 hours
Cost: $131 million
Use: Surveillance

Raven RQ-11
Wingspan: 4.5 feet (1.4 m)
Flight time: 1.5 hours
Cost: $35,000
Use: Surveillance

Pioneer RQ-2
Wingspan: 16.9 feet (5.2 m)
Flight time: 5 hours
Cost: $850,000
Use: Surveillance; target acquisition

HANDLING IMPORTANT JOBS

Robots must provide information to soldiers. Military robots use the latest cameras and sensors to do this. These let robots serve as the eyes for soldiers. Robots must provide clear pictures. This can be difficult for drones flying high above a battle zone. Companies have responded with powerful cameras and computer processors to relay this information. Relaying information instantly helps soldiers react much more quickly to dangerous situations. These changes help save soldiers' lives.

Robots perform dangerous tasks. They defuse bombs, find mines, and see if buildings are safe. They can also detect poison gas, which soldiers can't see or smell. Sometimes the robots fail or are damaged from bombs. They must be able to continue working or be easily fixed. Most military robots are very sturdy, and some have replaceable parts.

DESIGNING ROBOTS

BIGDOG: A SHORT-LIVED ROBOT

Some military robots must be quiet. A loud robot could give away soldiers' positions. This issue became a problem for a robot named BigDog. The robot had four legs and resembled a dog. That's how it got its name. BigDog was part of the Defense Advanced Research Projects Agency (DARPA). It was designed to carry loads across long distances for soldiers. But during testing, the military realized how noisy it was. The BigDog project was canceled.

CONQUERING TERRAIN CHALLENGES

Robots move in different ways, depending on their job. Some robots need to travel over rough ground. They may have tank-like tracks to let them climb over rubble. Other robots have four legs. Four legs give them more stability than two legs. Being stable is very important for military robots.

There is a benefit to making robots with two legs like humans. A robot with two legs would be able to

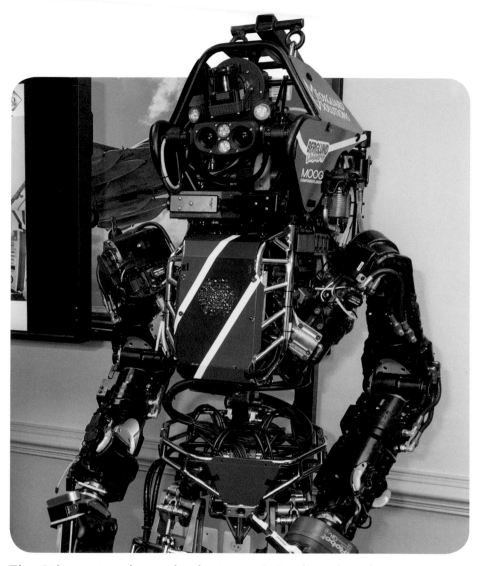

The Atlas, a two-legged robot, was introduced at the headquarters of the US Department of Defense in 2014.

walk through tight hallways. It could also interact with people more normally. For now, there are obstacles that two-legged robots have not overcome. They have trouble balancing on two legs. Some have trouble crouching, crawling, and standing up quickly.

AIR, LAND, AND SEA ROBOTS

Military robots carry out missions on land, in the air, and at sea. Each branch of the US military uses robots to do special jobs.

ROBOTS TAKE TO THE SKIES

UAVs provide scouting and armed attacks. The MQ-1 Predator changed the drone world. The Predator was designed in the 1990s to take pictures. Later, it was the first drone to carry missiles.

An MQ-9 Reaper drone sits on the runway in Berlin, Germany, in 2016.

SMALL DRONE, BIG RESPONSIBILITY

Some drones are really small. British soldiers use one called the Black Hornet. It looks like a tiny helicopter and can fit in the palm of a person's hand. The Black Hornet has three cameras. This makes it ideal for looking over walls or around corners. Because the drone is so small, the entire system can be carried by one soldier. The Black Hornet is not unique. Nano drones are becoming more popular.

The drone is flown remotely by a pilot. A second person operates the sensors and weapons. The Predator was phased out starting in 2017. It was replaced by the faster MQ-9 Reaper. The newer drone has better sensors and carries more weapons. The navy is looking at a system that shoots 30 small drones into the air. The small UAVs, called "nano drones," collect pictures and other information.

GROUND PATROLS

Unmanned ground vehicles (UGVs) perform jobs with troops on the ground. For example, the ACER, which stands for Armored Combat Engineer Robot, can

The Nakhlebnik unmanned combat ground vehicle was on display at a military show in Russia in 2017.

move heavy loads. It can carry 2,000 pounds (900 kg) or as much as an adult bull. It helps soldiers carry extra gear. A moving arm can lift approximately 900 pounds (400 kg) to help move cars or debris that are in the way.

Small UGVs are less than one foot (about 0.3 m) long. They move on tracks or wheels. Large UGVs

DESIGNING ROBOTS

ROBOTS MIMIC ANIMALS

Animals move easily through their environments. This is why robot designers often look to animals for inspiration. A US Navy robot is named GhostSwimmer. It looks and swims like a real fish. From a distance, it looks similar to a shark. The robot uses its tail to push itself forward and for control. It also has fins to help steer.

This robot looks like a small tank. It holds a lot of firepower in its compact size. MAARS has nonlethal lasers to blind the enemy. The SAFFiR, or Shipboard Autonomous Firefighting Robot, will be able to fight fires on ships. It is still in development. Advanced technology allows even small robots to send pictures or videos. Some are as small as an insect. This makes them much harder for an enemy to notice.

STRAIGHT TO THE
SOURCE

The military is facing challenges recruiting RPA (remotely piloted aircraft) pilots. The Government Accountability Office said in a report:

> *RPA pilots in 8 of the 10 focus groups we conducted reported that they found it rewarding to be able to contribute to combat operations every day. . . . RPA pilots also stated that they face multiple challenging working conditions including: long hours, working shifts that frequently rotate, and remaining in assignments beyond typical lengths.*
>
> *The Air Force may face challenges recruiting officers to serve as RPA pilots because of a negative perception that some in the Air Force associate with flying RPAs. . . . According to these officials one reason some view flying an RPA negatively is because flying an RPA does not require pilots to operate an aircraft while on board an aircraft in-flight.*
>
> Source: "Management of Unmanned Aerial System Pilot." *GAO.* GAO, April 2014. Web. Accessed October 18, 2017.

Back It Up

The author of this passage uses evidence to support a point. Write a paragraph describing this point. Then write down two or three pieces of evidence the author uses to make the point.

THE FUTURE OF MILITARY ROBOTS

The use of military robots is expected to continue. In 2016, the US military purchased 12,336 robots. By 2025, it is expected to buy more than 46,900 robots.

ROBOT WARS?

The latest technology gives militaries an advantage. That's why so many countries use robots. Soon soldiers could have wearable robotic parts to help do their jobs. This could even lead to a future in which battles are fought by robots.

The X-47B, a futuristic prototype drone, launched from and landed on an aircraft carrier in 2013.

INTELLIGENT ROBOTS

Artificial intelligence (AI) is the ability of computer systems to think like humans. This means they can learn and make decisions. AI can make military robots smarter and help identify targets. There are advantages, but there are problems too.

Some people warn against the dangers of AI. They include business leader Elon Musk and physicist Stephen Hawking. They believe that AI robots will cause a new arms race. Some people worry that if robots become too smart, they won't need humans. The main potential problem is if robots could learn on their own. They could then decide who to kill. This could even be innocent people.

ARTIFICIAL INTELLIGENCE

Artificial intelligence (AI) lets robots make decisions without humans. All military robots are controlled by humans. With AI, robots could decide when to fire a weapon. They could also determine the best route to reach a location. The Department of Defense is making AI part of its defense strategy.

US AIR FORCE PILOTS BY THE NUMBERS

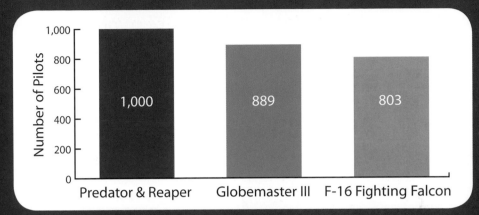

The Air Force had 1,000 remote pilot operators fly Predator and Reaper drones in 2017. That's more than the number of pilots who flew the Globemaster III transport plane or the F-16 Fighting Falcon fighter jet. What are the benefits of using UAVs over traditional airplanes? What downsides are there for not having a pilot in the cockpit?

In a worst-case scenario, AI robots could turn on the humans who created them.

MORE ROBOTS THAN SOLDIERS?

By the year 2025, the US military is expected to have more robots than humans. Many human jobs may be replaced. This would include driving cargo vehicles. These trucks could drive themselves.

Robots may also work together. Right now, an unmanned boat can relay a signal to an unmanned submarine. The sub would then launch a flying drone. This is the idea behind the Switchblade drone.

DESIGNING ROBOTS

WEARABLE ROBOTS

One way new technology could be used is to have human soldiers wear robotic gear. A project in development would connect to a soldier's leg. The robot's machinery lifts the person's leg. This allows him to run faster. The goal is to allow an average soldier to run one mile (1.6 km) in just four minutes.

ROBOTS TO THE RESCUE

Robots could soon be used to carry wounded soldiers to safety. Normally, medics treat injured soldiers in the warzone. This puts medics at risk. Many have been killed or injured helping others. With new technology, UGVs could scoop up soldiers and carry them to safety. Then medics could treat them.

AN IMPORTANT PART
OF THE MILITARY

From scouting to disabling bombs to carrying cargo, robots have become a critical part of the military. Robots have shown their value in both war and peacekeeping missions. They have saved countless lives. They have also made soldiers' jobs easier and less dangerous. As robot technology advances, robots will continue to support soldiers and prevent casualties.

EXPLORE ONLINE

Chapter Five talks about the future possibilities of military robots. What was one of the main points of the chapter? What evidence is included to support this point? Watch the video at the website below featuring robotics expert P. W. Singer. Does Singer bring up similar topics to those discussed in Chapter Five?

MILITARY ROBOTS AND THE FUTURE OF WAR
abdocorelibrary.com/military-robots

FAST FACTS

- Robots are operated or flown by a person with a remote control or other technology.

- All military robots today have some degree of human control.

- Experts around the world are studying autonomous military robots and their possible consequences.

- Leonardo da Vinci is credited with designing one of the first robots in the mid-1490s.

- Nikola Tesla invented the first remote-controlled device, a boat, in 1898.

- Leading Systems Inc. was awarded a $40 million contract to build the first modern drone in 1984.

- The military has about 7,500 drones, which is more than 40 percent of the military's aircraft.

- Robots are designed to handle specific jobs. That's why some fly, some go underwater, some have tracks like tanks, and others have arms like claws.

- The MQ-1 Predator has been called the drone that changed the world because of its ability to strike anywhere.

STOP AND
THINK

Say What?

Studying the military and technology can mean learning new words. Write five words or phrases in this book you've never heard before. Use a dictionary or the Internet to find out what they mean. Then write the meanings in your own words and use each word or phrase in a sentence.

Why Do I Care?

Maybe you don't know anyone who served in the military. However, think about others who have. How do robots help them and protect them? What would happen if they didn't have the robots? How would their jobs be different?

Take a Stand

The military relies on robots. They do dangerous jobs and save lives. Do you think all countries should be allowed to have military robots? Should countries that have them agree to limitations on how they can be used? Write a paragraph with reasons that support your opinion.

Tell the Tale

Chapter One starts with the story of a soldier who encounters a roadside bomb. Imagine you're in the army facing the same situation. Write 200 words describing why you would send a robot to dispose of the bomb rather than sending a soldier. What steps would you take to ensure everyone is safe?

GLOSSARY

arms race
a competition between two or more countries in developing advanced weapons

artificial intelligence
the ability of robots or machines to learn on their own

crouch
a lowered stance with the knees bent and the body leaned forward

obstacle
something that is in the way of an object's movement

peacekeeping
trying to avoid conflict

processor
the part of a computer that carries out instructions

remote-controlled
able to be operated from a distance

replaceable
when a new version can take the place of an older or damaged object

scout
a person or thing who gathers information for a larger group

warzone
an area where military combat is taking place

ONLINE RESOURCES

To learn more about military robots, visit our free resource websites below.

Visit **abdocorelibrary.com** for free Common Core resources for teachers and students, including vetted activities, multimedia, and booklinks, for deeper subject comprehension.

Visit **abdobooklinks.com** for free additional online weblinks for further learning. These links are routinely monitored and updated to provide the most current information available.

LEARN MORE

Drones: From Insect Spy Drones to Bomber Drones. New York: Scholastic, 2014.

Mooney, Carla. *Awesome Military Robots*. Minneapolis, MN: Abdo Publishing, 2015.

INDEX

About the Author

Brett S. Martin has more than 20 years of writing experience.
He has worked as a reporter, editor, director of public
relations, and president of his own media company. He
has written for more than two dozen magazines and has
written several fiction and nonfiction books. Martin lives in
Shakopee, Minnesota, with his wife and two teenage sons.